**Being in Government**

Fact Finders®

# So You Want to Be
# PRESIDENT
## OF THE UNITED STATES

by Elizabeth Pagel-Hogan

**Consultant:**
Fred Slocum,
Associate Professor of Political Science,
Minnesota State University, Mankato

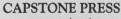

**CAPSTONE PRESS**
a capstone imprint

Fact Finders Books are published by Capstone Press
1710 Roe Crest Drive, North Mankato, Minnesota 56003
www.mycapstone.com

**Library of Congress Cataloging-in-Publication Data**
Names: Pagel-Hogan, Elizabeth, author.
Title: So you want to be President of the United States / by Elizabeth
   Pagel-Hogan.
Description: North Mankato, Minn. : Capstone Press, 2019. | Series: Being in
   government | Audience: Age 8–9. | Audience: Grade 4 to 6.
Identifiers: LCCN 2019004859| ISBN 9781543571943 (hardcover) | ISBN
   9781543575309 (paperback) | ISBN 9781543571981 (ebook pdf)
Subjects:  LCSH: Presidents—United States—Juvenile literature.
Classification: LCC JK517 .P34 2019 | DDC 352.23023/73—dc23
LC record available at https://lccn.loc.gov/2019004859

**Editorial Credits**
Mari Bolte, editor; Jennifer Bergstrom, designer;
Jo Miller, media researcher; Laura Manthe, production specialist

**Photo Credits**
iStockphoto: Steve Debenport, Cover; Newscom: AdMedia/CNP/Pool/Olivier Douliery, 18, Everett Collection, 8, KidStock Blend Images, 29, KRT/Paul Morse, 10, MEGA/CNP/Ron Sachs, 23, picture-alliance/dpa/Ron Sachs, 25, Polaris, 17, Roll Call Photos/File Photo, 25, Win McNamee - Pool via CNP, 14, World History Archive, 20, ZUMA Press/Allen Jr., Willie J., 27, ZUMA Press/Damon Higgins, 28, ZUMA Press/Pete Souza, 13; Shutterstock: JPL Designs, 7, Luca Perra, 5, Rob Crandall, 15, 19; Wikimedia: Library of Congress Prints and Photographs, 24

**Design Elements**
Capstone; Shutterstock: primiaou, Rebellion Works, simbos, Yes - Royalty Free

# TABLE OF CONTENTS

Chapter 1

**WANTED: COMMANDER
IN CHIEF** ◄ 4

Chapter 2

**GET ALL THE DETAILS** ◄ 6

Chapter 3

**THE PRESIDENT
AS A ROLE MODEL** ◄ 12

Chapter 4

**THE PRESIDENT
ON THE HOME FRONT** ◄ 14

Chapter 5

**SOUND LIKE FUN?** ◄ 26

**GLOSSARY** ◄ 30

**READ MORE** ◄ 31

**CRITICAL THINKING QUESTIONS** ◄ 31

**INTERNET SITES** ◄ 31

**INDEX** ◄ 32

# WANTED:
## COMMANDER IN CHIEF

Are you a leader who likes to solve problems? Can you give a great speech that inspires and motivates people? Do you like meeting people from around the world?

If your answers are yes, you could be a great candidate for president of the United States of America (also known as POTUS).

Must be:
- ✓ at least 35 years old
- ✓ an American citizen born in the United States
- ✓ a U.S. resident for the past 14 years

Successful candidates move to Washington, D.C., and live in the White House. All expenses are paid. A private bowling alley, swimming pool, and movie theater are included with your new home.

This is a 24-hour-a-day job that also requires extensive travel around the world. Since this is also a dangerous job, safety and security are provided by the Secret Service.

The White House has 132 rooms, three kitchens, and 35 bathrooms.

# Chapter 2

# GET ALL
# THE DETAILS

The role of the president is one of three parts of the U.S. government. The president, vice president, and the president's Cabinet are part of the **executive** branch. The other two branches are the **legislative** and **judicial**. The legislative branch is Congress, which includes the Senate and House of Representatives. The judicial branch is the Supreme Court and other federal courts.

The president is not a king or queen. There are limits on the president's power. The U.S. government has a system of checks and balances. Checks and balances make sure that no one part of the government has more control than another part. This is why the government has three branches. Each branch can change or block the actions of the other branches.

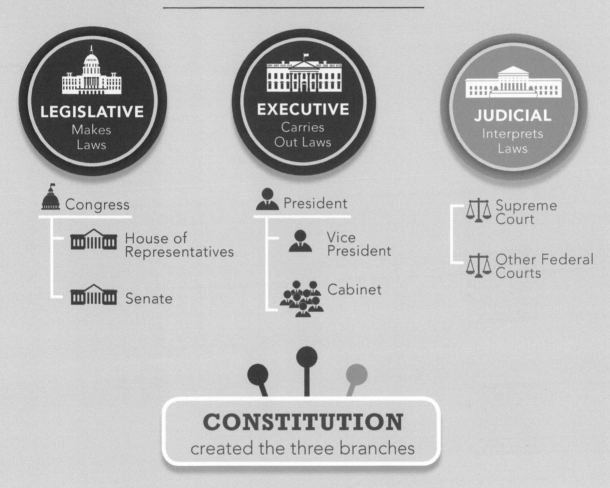

# ★ THE ★ THREE BRANCHES OF GOVERNMENT

**LEGISLATIVE**
Makes Laws

**EXECUTIVE**
Carries Out Laws

**JUDICIAL**
Interprets Laws

Congress
— House of Representatives
— Senate

President
— Vice President
— Cabinet

Supreme Court
Other Federal Courts

**CONSTITUTION**
created the three branches

**executive branch**—the part of government that makes sure the laws are obeyed

**judicial branch**—the part of government that explains laws

**legislative branch**—the part of government that passes bills that become laws

A president is elected to serve a four-year term. Citizens vote for their choice of president on a Tuesday in early November. The candidate with a majority of electoral votes wins the election. In January, two months after being elected, the president-elect attends the **inaugural** ceremony and takes the oath of office.

**FACT:** The law allows for a president to be **impeached** by the House and convicted by the Senate before his or her term is finished. If this were to happen, that person would have to leave the presidency. Two presidents have been impeached, but neither was convicted. One other president resigned rather than face probable impeachment.

*"I do solemnly swear (or affirm) that I will faithfully execute the Office of president of the United States, and will to the best of my Ability, preserve, protect, and defend the Constitution of the United States."*
—*the Presidential Oath of Office*

# POPULARITY CONTEST

Not every president wins the popular vote. Citizens cast votes for their favorite candidate, but according to the Constitution, electors from each state vote for the candidate from the party that won their state. Five candidates who did not win the popular vote have become president. These candidates were John Quincy Adams in 1824, Rutherford B. Hayes in 1876, Benjamin Harrison in 1888, George W. Bush in 2000, and Donald Trump in 2016.

The first president, George Washington, only served two four-year terms. He created a model that other presidents followed. However, Franklin D. Roosevelt was elected four times—in 1932, 1936, 1940, and 1944. He died in office in 1945. In 1947 Congress passed the 22nd Amendment, which officially limited presidents to two terms. It was **ratified** in 1951.

**impeach**—charge an elected official with a serious crime; it can result in removal from office

**inaugural**—swearing in

**ratify**—formally approve

In 1909 President William Howard Taft hired an architect to build a presidential office. The Oval Office is modeled after the Blue Room, one of the parlors on the first floor of the White House.

Being president isn't like a regular job where a person works for eight hours and then goes home. The president lives and works in the White House. His or her family, known as the first family, lives with the president on the second floor. The Oval Office, which is in the West Wing, is where work is done.

# THEY PAY FOR WHAT?

The president has to buy his or her own clothes, snacks, dry cleaning, and meals. He or she also pays for any private events and activities. Midnight pizza deliveries—and delivery driver tips—are personal expenses that come out of the president's pocket.

The president is paid a salary of $400,000 every year. He or she also receives $50,000 for expenses and $100,000 to spend on official travel. The president also gets an entertainment allowance of $19,000 a year. Congress decides how much money the president is paid. The president can't give himself or herself a raise.

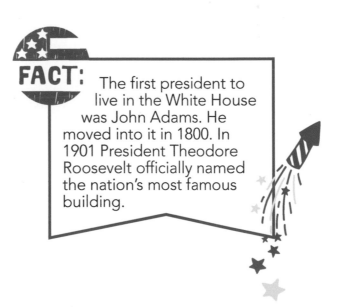

**FACT:** The first president to live in the White House was John Adams. He moved into it in 1800. In 1901 President Theodore Roosevelt officially named the nation's most famous building.

11

# THE PRESIDENT AS A ROLE MODEL

The president is very busy and has a lot of duties and responsibilities. As the chief citizen of the United States, the president should set an example for the country with his or her choices and behavior while in public.

Visits to schools, community centers, and national parks encourage everyone in the country to appreciate special people and places. Teachers, scientists, and even students have their hard work and achievements honored by the president.

Sometimes events are special or exciting. The president may meet with award-winning authors and artists, congratulate sports teams on their victories, or appear on late-night TV talk shows.

In 2008 President Barack Obama began holding a Passover seder for friends and staff. He hosted a seder every year he served in the White House.

The president does get to have fun. Throwing out the first pitch at baseball games, hosting movie nights at the White House, or challenging members of Congress to basketball games are only a few of the activities past presidents have chosen. The president's family hosts Easter egg hunts in the spring and trick-or-treating at Halloween. At Thanksgiving, a turkey is pardoned.

## WHAT'S NEXT?

Many presidents stay busy after they leave office. George Washington returned to farming. William Howard Taft became a Supreme Court justice. Modern leaders usually help create their presidential libraries. They write books about their time in office. They give inspirational speeches. Many are involved in charities. Past presidents George H.W. Bush (who died in 2018) and Bill Clinton worked together to raise money to help people after a tsunami in southeast Asia in 2004.

13

# Chapter 4

# THE PRESIDENT ON THE HOME FRONT

The president needs to know what's going on in all of the states and territories. He or she does that by talking to leaders and citizens around the country. Every year, the president gives a speech to Congress called the State of the Union. This speech tells Congress how the country is doing. In this speech, the president also talks about plans for the coming year. This speech is televised so everyone in the U.S. can hear from the president.

President Bill Clinton was the first president to live-stream the State of the Union on the internet.

President George W. Bush gave the State of the Union address in front of Congress in 2005.

# JOBS AND TITLES

The president has many roles and titles. Some include:
> commander in chief: leading the military
> chief executive: leading the government
> chief administrative officer: ensuring the laws are upheld
> chief diplomat: representing the country to the rest of the world
> ceremonial head of state: performing symbolic duties

## The Cabinet

Someone has to make sure laws are followed. Even though the president is in charge, there are a lot of things to keep track of! So the president picks people to help with this job. They are part of the president's Cabinet. In most Cabinet agencies, the person in charge is called a secretary. Each Cabinet secretary has a different role. One secretary pays attention to education. Others are in charge of defense or housing. The vice president is part of the Cabinet too.

There are also government agencies outside the cabinet that help keep our country running. Some of these agencies are the Environmental Protection Agency, the Social Security Administration, and the Central Intelligence Agency. The president picks people to lead them, and the Senate approves them. They are called secretaries, directors, or administrators. These officials follow the president's ideas and guidelines on how to run the country and enforce the laws.

# MEMBERS OF THE CABINET

There are 16 positions in the president's Cabinet. They are:

> vice president
> secretary of state
> secretary of the treasury
> secretary of defense
> attorney general
   (leads the Department
   of Justice)
> secretary of the interior
> secretary of agriculture
> secretary of commerce

> secretary of labor
> secretary of health
   and human services
> secretary of housing
   and urban development
> secretary of transportation
> secretary of energy
> secretary of education
> secretary of veterans affairs
> secretary of homeland security

President Donald Trump and his Cabinet, 2018.

Former presidents Bill Clinton and Barack Obama visited an office building together in 2011. They were encouraging energy cost cutting and the hiring of construction jobs.

## How Is Everyone Doing?

A strong country needs a strong **economy**. The president needs to know if businesses—both big **corporations** and small family-owned stores—are doing well. Are there enough jobs? Are people struggling to find work? Meeting with government agencies, business leaders, and ordinary citizens helps the president answer these questions.

The president also thinks about **taxes**. With Congress's help, he or she decides if taxes are too low or too high. Lowering taxes can help the economy grow. Raising them can help pay for things such as defense, health care, or education.

## FACT: PICTURES ON PAPER

Some presidents have been honored with a place on U.S. currency after their death. George Washington, Abraham Lincoln, Andrew Jackson, Ulysses S. Grant, and Thomas Jefferson are presidents who show up on bills and coins. No living people are shown on U.S. money.

Andrew Jackson, Ulysses S. Grant, Benjamin Franklin, Thomas Jefferson, and Abraham Lincoln are some of the people on U.S. bills. Franklin is the only non-president.

**corporations**—companies formed by law and having certain legal duties

**economy**—the way a country produces, distributes, and uses its money, goods, natural resources, and services

**taxes**—money collected from a country's citizens to help pay for running the government

## Who Makes the Rules?

Although the president makes sure laws are followed, he or she does not make the laws. Congress passes bills and sends them to the president. The president either signs the bills into law or **vetoes** them. If Congress really wants that law to be passed, though, they can override a veto. Two-thirds of all senators and representatives must agree to override a vetoed bill.

Franklin D. Roosevelt signed 3,721 executive orders during his four terms as president. This is more than any other president.

The president can ask Congress to pass certain laws. The president might make a speech or meet with senators and representatives to persuade them to do so.

Executive orders are policies that can be written by the president. They do not need to be approved by Congress. This means there isn't a lot of debate about the good and bad parts of an executive order. And they have to be followed, just like laws. But judges can overturn executive orders if they go against the Constitution. Orders can also be changed or overturned by the next president.

## THEY DID WHAT?

Many important laws in the nation are executive orders issued by presidents. Some significant orders include:

> the Emancipation Proclamation of 1863, written by Abraham Lincoln
> the first national monument, Devil's Tower in Wyoming, signed into order by Theodore Roosevelt in 1906
> the imprisonment of Japanese American citizens during World War II (1935–1945), issued by Franklin Delano Roosevelt in 1942

veto—presidential power to reject a bill passed by Congress

# Global Leader

The president is the leader of the United States Armed Forces, which includes the Army, Navy, Air Force, Marine Corps, and Coast Guard. The military protects the country under the president's direction. The president cannot declare war on another country. Only Congress can do that. But the president can send the military to handle dangerous situations around the globe.

Ambassadors are chosen by the president to represent the United States in other nations. They work with leaders of other countries to build relationships abroad.

Other countries' leaders also meet with the president. Sometimes the visits are fun, with fancy parties to greet foreign **dignitaries** or ceremonies to honor people or events. Other times they are serious meetings about difficult topics. The president has to be ready for all kinds of visits.

The president signs **treaties** between the United States and other nations. Treaty subjects might include trade agreements, arms control, or human rights. The Senate must ratify any treaty the president signs.

George H.W. Bush and his military advisors at the Pentagon in 1990.

**dignitary**—a person who holds a position of respect or honor
**treaty**—a formal agreement between groups or nations

## Party Leader

Political parties are organized groups of people who have ideas about how to run the country. In the modern United States, there are two main political parties—the Democratic Party and the Republican Party. There are also other smaller groups, called third parties. The Libertarian Party and the Green Party are examples of third parties.

Presidential candidates are nominated by their parties. Elected presidents endorse political candidates. They might make speeches in support of candidates with similar views. The president also chooses people from his or her party to work in the Cabinet.

## FIRST WOMEN

Belva Ann Lockwood
(1830–1917)

Belva Ann Lockwood was the first woman candidate of any party. She went to law school and persuaded Congress to pass a law in 1879 allowing her to practice before the U.S. Supreme Court. She received the nomination of the Equal Rights Party in 1884.

The first woman candidate of a major party was Margaret Chase Smith, a Republican senator from Maine. She announced her candidacy at the Women's National Press Club on January 27, 1964. She was already the first woman to serve in both houses of Congress. Unfortunately, she lost the nomination.

In 1968 Charlene Mitchell ran for president as a candidate of the Communist Party. She was both the first black female candidate for president and the first woman to head a minor party ticket in the 20th century.

Also in 1968, Shirley Chisholm became the first African American woman in Congress. In addition, she was the first black woman to seek a presidential nomination from a major political party during the 1972 election.

Shirley Chisholm
(1924–2005)

In 2016 Hillary Clinton was the first woman to win the presidential nomination of a major political party. She was already the only first lady to win a public office seat when she was elected to the Senate in 2001. She lost the general election in November 2016.

Hillary Clinton
(1947–   )

# SOUND LIKE FUN?

Do the duties of the president sound great? Although you'll have to wait until you turn 35 to be elected, there are many ways you can practice being president now.

If your school has a student council, consider running for office. This will help you get comfortable making speeches. It will also give you practice being a leader. You don't have to run only for president. Running for other offices can help you learn how the entire system works. But get ready for hard work! Student council is a big job no matter what position you choose.

Take it to the next level and attend a school board or PTA meeting. Getting knowledgeable about programs that directly affect you is a great first step in making change.

Nearly 1 million kids learned about the election process by casting their votes through their schools and online during the 2016 election.

Volunteering is a great way to learn the skills a president needs. You may have to work with a team of people to get a job done. Being a volunteer is a great chance to learn how to work with others. When you volunteer, pay attention to how the leader of the group acts. See how he or she encourages people, and borrow some of those techniques yourself.

Learn the history of your country by visiting a library. History will tell you how events played out and where mistakes were made. That information, both good and bad, can help you make smart decisions in the future.

Take a look at your community. Is there something that you think needs to be changed? Maybe there is something good that could be created. Send a letter or email to community leaders. Explain what you think needs to be done. Then offer ideas or suggestions about how it could be accomplished.

Find your local or state politicians on social media. This is an easy way to stay updated with their latest schedules, votes, and opinions. Attend city council or town hall meetings, which give citizens the opportunity to speak in front of those politicians.

Middle schoolers lined up to register to vote in their school's mock election.

Read, ask questions, and speak up! Your voice deserves to be heard.

Listen to people who have ideas different from yours. A president needs to work with members of the Cabinet, members of Congress, and people from across the nation. The president also needs to think about how policies affect all U.S. citizens. Each of these groups will have different ideas. Being president means listening to different ideas and working together.

You're on your way to the presidency!

# GLOSSARY

**corporations** (KOR-puh-ray-shuhns)—companies formed by law and having certain legal duties

**Democratic Party** (de-muh-KRA-tik PAR-tee)—one of the two major parties in the United States; Democrats are viewed as more progressive, supporting social and economic equality. They also believe the government should use more control with the economy, but less in private affairs.

**dignitary** (DIG-nuh-tehr-ee)—a person who holds a position of respect or honor

**economy** (i-KAH-nuh-mee)—the way a country produces, distributes, and uses its money, goods, natural resources, and services

**executive branch** (ig-ZE-kyuh-tiv BRANCH)—to do with the branch of government that makes sure the laws are obeyed

**impeach** (im-PEECH)—charge an elected official with a serious crime; it can result in removal from office

**inaugural** (in-AW-ger-ul)—swearing in; the beginning of a period of office

**judicial branch** (joo-DISH-uhl BRANCH)—the part of government that explains laws

**legislative branch** (LEJ-iss-lay-tiv BRANCH)—the part of government that passes bills that become laws

**ratify** (RAT-if-eye)—formally approve

**Republican Party** (ri-PUHB-lik-uhn PAR-tee)—one of the two major parties in the United States. They believe in conservative social policies, low taxes, and believe that the government should stay out of the economy.

**taxes** (TAKS-uhs)—money collected from a country's citizens to help pay for running the government

**treaty** (TREE-tee)—a formal agreement between groups or nations

**veto** (VEE-toh)—presidential power to reject a bill passed by Congress; if two-thirds of both houses pass the bill again, they override the veto, and the bill becomes law

# READ MORE

**Gonzales, Debbie.** *Girls With Guts!: The Road to Breaking Barriers and Bashing Records.* Watertown, MA: Charlesbridge, 2018.

**Goodwin, Susan E.** *See How They Run: Campaign Dreams, Election Schemes, and the Race to the White House.* New York: Bloomsbury, 2019.

**Murray, Julie.** *President.* My Government. Minneapolis, MN: ABDO Kids, 2018.

# CRITICAL THINKING QUESTIONS

1. Think about the checks and balances in our government. If we had a king or queen instead of a president, how would our government work differently?
2. The president is called the chief of party. But sometimes the president selects people from different parties to run different agencies and commissions. What are the pros and cons of this?
3. What are the benefits of the president issuing executive orders? What are the drawbacks?

# INTERNET SITES

*Chronological List of Presidents, First Ladies, and Vice Presidents of the United States*
https://www.loc.gov/rr/print/list/057_chron.html

*Presidents*
https://www.whitehouse.gov/about-the-white-house/presidents

*Presidents, Vice Presidents, and First Ladies of the United States*
https://www.usa.gov/presidents

# INDEX

Adams, John, 11
Adams, John Quincy, 9
ambassadors, 22
amendments, 9

bills, 20
Bush, George H.W., 13, 23
Bush, George W., 9, 15

Cabinet, 6, 16, 17, 24, 29
Chisholm, Shirley, 25
Clinton, Bill, 13, 14, 18
Clinton, Hillary, 25
Congress, 6, 9, 11, 13, 14, 15,
   19, 20, 21, 22, 24, 25, 29
Constitution, 9, 21

elections, 8, 9, 24, 25, 26, 27, 28
Emancipation Proclamation, 21
executive branch, 6
executive orders, 20, 21

Grant, Ulysses S., 19

Harrison, Benjamin, 9
Hayes, Rutherford B., 9
House of Representatives, 6, 8

impeachment, 8

Jackson, Andrew, 19
Jefferson, Thomas, 19
judicial branch, 6

legislative branch, 6
Lincoln, Abraham, 19, 21

Lockwood, Belva Ann, 24

Mitchell, Charlene, 25

Obama, Barack, 13, 18

Pentagon, 23
political parties, 24, 25

Roosevelt, Franklin Delano, 9, 20, 21
Roosevelt, Theodore, 11, 21

salary, 11
Secret Service, 4
Senate, 8, 16, 25
Smith, Margaret Chase, 25
State of the Union, 14, 15
Supreme Court, 6, 13, 24

Taft, William Howard, 10, 13
taxes, 19
terms, 8, 9
treaties, 22
Trump, Donald, 9, 17

United States Armed Forces, 22

vice president, 6
voting, 8, 9, 27, 28

Washington, George, 9, 19
White House, 4, 5, 10, 11, 13
   Oval Office, 10
   West Wing, 10